Get Motoring!
Trains

by Dalton Rains

www.focusreaders.com

Copyright © 2024 by Focus Readers®, Mendota Heights, MN 55120. All rights reserved. No part of this book may be reproduced or utilized in any form or by any means without written permission from the publisher.

Focus Readers is distributed by North Star Editions:
sales@northstareditions.com | 888-417-0195

Produced for Focus Readers by Red Line Editorial.

Photographs ©: Shutterstock Images, cover, 1, 4 (top), 4 (bottom), 7, 9, 11, 13, 15 (top), 15 (bottom), 16 (top left), 16 (top right), 16 (bottom left), 16 (bottom right)

Library of Congress Cataloging-in-Publication Data
Names: Rains, Dalton, author.
Title: Trains / by Dalton Rains.
Description: Mendota Heights, MN : Focus Readers, [2024] | Series: Get
  motoring! | Includes index. | Audience: Grades K-1
Identifiers: LCCN 2023033088 (print) | LCCN 2023033089 (ebook) | ISBN
  9798889980117 (hardcover) | ISBN 9798889980544 (paperback) | ISBN
  9798889981398 (pdf) | ISBN 9798889980971 (ebook)
Subjects: LCSH: Railroad trains--Juvenile literature. | Railroad
  trains--Parts--Juvenile literature. | CYAC: Railroad trains. | LCGFT:
  Instructional and educational works.
Classification: LCC TF148 .R35 2024 (print) | LCC TF148 (ebook) | DDC
  625.2--dc23/eng/20230731
LC record available at https://lccn.loc.gov/2023033088
LC ebook record available at https://lccn.loc.gov/2023033089

Printed in the United States of America
Mankato, MN
012024

About the Author

Dalton Rains is a writer and editor who lives in Minnesota.

Table of Contents

Trains 5

Parts 6

Uses 12

Glossary 16

Index 16

rails

cargo

Trains

Trains move on **rails**.

They can carry people

or **cargo**.

Many trains are very long.

Parts

Most trains have an engine.

The engine has bright lights.

It also has a loud horn.

The horn lets people know

the train is near.

There are many cars in a train.

The engine pulls the cars.

A **coupler** connects two

cars together.

A passenger car carries people.

A tank car carries **liquid**.

A boxcar carries many kinds
of goods.

Uses

Railways connect train stations together. Trains move from one station to another.

Some trains move cargo

a long way.

Other trains stay in one city.

Glossary

cargo

liquid

coupler

rails

Index

E
engine, 6, 8

G
goods, 10

H
horn, 6

S
stations, 12